CAMPFIRE COOKING

CAMPFIRE COOKING

MOUTHWATERING SKILLET, DUTCH OVEN, AND SKEWER RECIPES

Jakob Nusbaum

Translated by Rita McMaster

Photos by Jesper Rais

Skyhorse Publishing

Skyhorse Publishing books may be purchased in bulk at special discounts for sales promotion, corporate gifts, fund-raising, or educational purposes. Special editions can also be created to specifications. For details, contact the Special Sales Department, Skyhorse Publishing, 307 West 36th Street, 11th Floor, New York, NY 10018 or info@skyhorsepublishing.com.

Skyhorse® and Skyhorse Publishing® are registered trademarks of Skyhorse Publishing, Inc.®, a Delaware corporation.

Visit our website at www.skyhorsepublishing.com.

10 9 8 7 6 5 4 3 2 1

Library of Congress Cataloging-in-Publication Data

Names: Nusbaum, Jakob, author. | Rais, Jesper, photographer.
Title: Campfire cooking : mouthwatering skillet, Dutch oven, and skewer recipes / Jakob Nusbaum ; photos by Jesper Rais.
Other titles: Brændende kærlighed. English
Description: New York, NY : Skyhorse Publishing, [2023] | "Originally published by Turbine forlaget in 2021 under the title Brændende kærlighed." | Summary: "50 mouthwatering recipes to enjoy around the campfire"-- Provided by publisher.
Identifiers: LCCN 2022050976 (print) | LCCN 2022050977 (ebook) | ISBN 9781510774902 (hardcover) | ISBN 9781510775299 (epub)
Subjects: LCSH: Outdoor cooking. | Dutch oven cooking. | Skillet cooking. | LCGFT: Cookbooks.
Classification: LCC TX823 .N8713 2023 (print) | LCC TX823 (ebook) | DDC 641.5/782--dc23/eng/20221109
LC record available at https://lccn.loc.gov/2022050976
LC ebook record available at https://lccn.loc.gov/2022050977

Cover design by David Ter-Avanesyan
Cover and interior photos by Jesper Rais
Illustrations by Jimi Holstebro, HoedtHolstebro
Graphic design by Karin Hald

Print ISBN: 978-1-5107-7490-2
Ebook ISBN: 978-1-5107-7529-9

Printed in China

Page 50

Page 58

Page 79

Page 90

Page 102

CONTENTS

Page 120

Page 130

Page 142

Page 148

Page 156

MAINS

DESSERTS

DRINKS

CONDIMENTS

JAKOB:

- Father of two boys
- Former art director
- Hunter and fly fisherman

FOR THE LOVE OF CAMPFIRES

This cookbook is for those of you who love the idea of cooking outdoors.

You may already have invested in new equipment—or you're planning to do so—but like so many others, you may have stopped short of actually going outdoors to cook on a real campfire. I hope my easy and delicious recipes as well as my tips and tricks will help you get over the last hurdle and start cooking outdoors.

It's all about keeping it simple, especially at first. You're even allowed to cheat a little. It's better to make a stew at home and take it out into nature to heat up over a campfire, than not to go out at all.

The goal is to enjoy time together around the campfire and to experience how much fun it is to eat outdoors. This book will guide you through how to start a fire, how to take care of your fire, and how to make cooking over a campfire a great success.

If you're already used to cooking over an open fire, I urge you to use this book as a source of inspiration and new ideas. Knowing the technique behind a recipe is key, and it's therefore a good idea—at least in the beginning—to follow the recipes exactly. However, my aim is also to give you the confidence to alter the recipes to your liking and to experiment with new ingredients. If there are any vegetables or other ingredients that "speak" to you, then you should use them. Once you know what you're doing, it's your right to follow your very own outdoor cooking rules.

We all have very busy lives and are surrounded by the constant buzz of apps, alarms, electronic gadgets, and social media. We're on 24/7. When we cook over a campfire, we need to disconnect and be present to focus on the cooking 100 percent, because otherwise the food will burn, or the fire will go out and we'll have to start over. Cooking together over a campfire is a wonderful experience. The tranquility of nature, building a fire with friends or family, the smell of food cooking, even getting smoke in your eyes—it's magic.

I have created Outdoor Team Cooking events for industry leaders and for employees in private companies for several years. The participants have even been involved in butchering wild boars, deer, or sheep, and have prepared oysters over a fire. I love big, elaborate campfire projects where roasts have to be grilled slowly over embers for many hours. It's like therapy for me to cook this way. Taking care of the fire throughout the process is an important part of the job. At NorthSide music festival in Denmark, we used to have 20 skewers cooking at the same time, each holding a pork roast that weighed 10–12 pounds. The sight and the smell of this was unforgettable.

But a fire doesn't have to be big to be wonderful, and you don't have to start out making feasts. Just start somewhere. My sincere hope is that this cookbook will help you get outside to cook more often and that you will have many great moments in nature by the fire.

See you by the campfire!

Jakob Nusbaum, Outdoor Cook & Founder of GOURMENSCH

THINGS TO GATHER FOR CAMPFIRE COOKING

// FOR THE FIRE

- Dry firewood, fire starters, matches or a long lighter
- Small kindling that you can buy from your hardware store or log dealer, or you can chop to size yourself
- Good fireproof gloves
- A shovel or stick for moving the firewood and charcoal around the campfire
- A bucket of water to put out the fire and for handwashing

// EQUIPMENT

- A pot or pan with a lid, a skillet, a grate and/or camp grill (many campsites already have grates that you can use)
- Long metal tongs for turning meat or vegetables on the fire
- A cutting board and a knife
- A pot and a ladle if you are making soup or a stew
- A sharp kitchen knife for slicing bread
- Cups, plates, forks, and knives (and/or spoons if you're making soup or stew)
- Napkins or kitchen towel

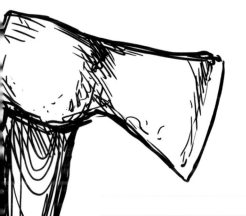

// WHAT TO BRING

- Cooler with icepacks for storing all perishables such as milk products, meat, fish, or shellfish
- Thermos with coffee or tea
- Beer or wine
- Water for drinking while you cook

// CLEANLINESS / HYGIENE

- Soap or other hand cleaner
- Kitchen towel
- Dishwashing liquid and a sponge
- Tea towels
- Dish cloths
- Garbage bags

// SAFETY

- Water for extinguishing the fire
- Band-Aids for if you happen to cut yourself
- Remember to check yourself as well as your friends and family for ticks after you've been outside in nature!

HOW TO START A CAMPFIRE AND KEEP IT BURNING

- Make sure your firewood is dry before you start a fire. Damp firewood produces a lot of smoke.

- Make sure that you have plenty of small kindling to start the fire. You can buy kindling and fire starters in hardware stores or at some gas stations.

INSTRUCTIONS FOR SAFE LOG SPLITTING
Safety note: if you're not comfortable splitting logs, you can buy logs that are already prepared for use on a campfire.

Place your log straight up toward the back of a sturdy chopping block. If you miss the log, you will cut into the chopping block and avoid injury to your legs. Make sure you spread your legs and that you raise the axe above your head before you chop. If the log can't stand on its own, **DO NOT** hold it with your hands or ask someone else to hold it for you as this could lead to serious injury. You can safely use an additional block of wood to support the log to make it stand up.

CAMPFIRE SITE
If there's not a ready-made campfire site or fire pit available, you can build your own campfire. Place a circle of stones around the area where you want to build a fire and use a shovel to remove any flammable material such as grass, turf, or leaves.

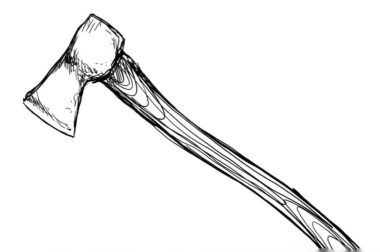

PAGODA FIRE

There are many ways and techniques to build a fire. The most important thing is that you can get it started. I usually start with a "pagoda" style fire, which produces great embers for cooking campfire food.

The way to build a pagoda fire is simply to place pieces of firewood in pairs in a square. The first four pieces are placed on the ground, and then you stack firewood on top until you have a square tower of firewood. Place the fire starters at the bottom, and if it's windy, you can place a larger piece of firewood on the top to give some cover from the wind. Place some slightly thicker pieces of firewood in the top part of the pagoda fire.

KEEPING THE FIRE BURNING

Keep in mind that you need to keep the fire burning by adding more firewood as you go. It's no fun having to restart your fire when your stomach is rumbling.

Embers are needed for grilling meat, vegetables, fish, bread on a stick, and marshmallows. Bear in mind that it takes about 2 hours to produce good embers on an open fire.

Fire is needed for cooking stews and soups. If you cook with fire, you need to make sure that you keep feeding your fire with small firewood under a pot or casserole. It's easier to control a fire with small pieces of firewood, which catch fire more quickly than larger pieces.

It's very helpful if you can adjust your cooking pot either up or down depending on the heat of your campfire, or if the pot can be moved to stand on a grate if the fire is too strong.

If you're making bread on a stick and need embers and are grilling meat or vegetables on a grate and need to keep a fire going at the same time, then you can divide the campfire into two parts with embers on one side and a fire on the other side. Use a shovel or a stick to move the logs or embers around.

REMEMBER TO EXTINGUISH THE FIRE WHEN YOU'E DONE

It's very important to think about safety by the campfire. A campfire can burn for many hours unless it's extinguished properly, and if the wind suddenly picks up, the embers can light up and you can have a disaster on your hands. Please always remember to have water on hand for extinguishing the campfire when you're finished making your meal. Be careful when you pour water over the fire because hot steam can rise from the embers.

And don't forget to clean up after yourself. Take your garbage home to allow the next user to have a nice experience by the fire. I usually tell my kids that when you leave a campfire, there should be no signs left to show that you've been there.

TIPS AND TRICKS FOR GETTING STARTED

- The easiest thing to cook over a campfire is a stew or a soup. You just need a pot and a skillet and a few ingredients. Bingo! And to make it even simpler, you can prep all the ingredients ahead of time at home.

  If you plan to grill something over the fire, you need to make sure the embers are hot and glowing, and keep in mind that it takes a couple of hours to produce perfect embers for cooking. If you plan to make a soup or a stew, you can make a small fire and start cooking right away. Make sure that the food is not overheated. You can very easily increase the heat from a fire but it's much harder to turn the down the heat. Should your pot become overheated, you can simply hoist it higher up away from the fire. You can also place the pot on a grate away from the fire. Another way to reduce the heat is to use a stick to move the logs away from your cooking pot.

- Make cooking your dinner quality time by inviting your family or friends out into nature to make the meal together. It doesn't have to be a huge project. In the summertime, I take a camp grill to the beach. The kids are playing on the beach while I start the fire and make something simple for dinner. Then we eat together and end our dinner with a swim. It's a great way to spend a few hours with family and friends. If you can find a campfire site with a grate, tables, and benches, then it's even easier to get started.

- It's OK to "cheat" by preparing things at home. It's perfectly fine to chop and slice the vegetables at home or prepare the meat so that all you have left to do is to combine all the ingredients in a warm pot over the fire. You can also prepare dressings or sides at home.

- Making a stew at home and heating it over the campfire works well if you would like to make things easy. You'll still have great fun and smoke in your eyes, which is not possible at the dinner table at home.

- If you're a beginner, then find an easy recipe and make it as simple as possible to avoid bringing too many things with you out into nature. Later, when you're more established as an outdoor cook, you can be more ambitious with your cooking.

SECRETS FOR SUCCESS

You won't master campfire cooking in one day, but you don't have to be really experienced to enjoy the taste of food made outdoors. Start by making simple dishes that you're comfortable with. The worst that could happen is that you burn the food. It happens to everyone from time to time. It may be a good idea to make a few extras of things like baked potatoes or baked apples or bananas, just in case one or two burn too much to be enjoyed. Over the years I have many burned steaks on my conscience because I left them on the embers too long. However, it doesn't matter if the food is just a little overcooked or burnt—it still tastes fantastic when you eat it outdoors. The smoke, the smell, the sounds, and the heat . . . all our senses are awakened outdoors by the fire.

I love to grill meat, vegetables, and fish on a grate over the fire. Cooking this way gives the food a smokiness that's hard to beat. The fat from the meat drips down into the fire and flares up suddenly to "kiss" the meat and give it extra love. In theory you can make the same food outdoors that you can make in the comfort of your home. This campfire cookbook explains the simple techniques that will allow you to get started quickly so you can enjoy quality time with those you love and enjoy the taste of food made on fire. If you'd like to add some extra taste to your vegetables, you can grill the vegetables over a grate before you add them into your casserole dish or soup. And if you're making a salad, try to grill as many of the vegetables as possible to make your salad extra delicious.

When my boys were young, they were given their own pots so that they could make soup or a stew over the campfire themselves. While I was grilling whole chickens or lamb, they made the first course. This made them feel part of the process, and they were able to decide what they wanted to cook in their pots. One time they asked if they could make Nettle Soup. We didn't have any root vegetables, greens, or stock, so I didn't think it would work. But the kids were so motivated that they went ahead without these ingredients and were happy with the result even though it wasn't exactly like a soup. It was more like nettle tea and with a little added sugar it was a great success. If I had stopped them from making the soup, they would not have had the experience of cooking "soup" outdoors for the first time, and we would not have had a chance to taste their special campfire tea.

RECIPES

All the recipes are for 4 people, unless otherwise noted.

Remember to grill meat, fish, vegetables, eggs, etc. over a grate over embers, avoiding large flames. If you are making a casserole dish or soups, then it's fine to have some flames under your cooking pot.

BREAKFAST

FRIED EGG TOAST WITH MUSHROOMS

This breakfast is easy and delicious. If you don't have access to large slices of bread that have room for 2 eggs, then make each piece of toast with one egg only. I like to toast the bread and the mushrooms until they become crispy.

// INGREDIENTS

½ pound (250 g) mushrooms
   (regular field mushrooms)
Butter for frying
Fresh thyme
4 large slices French-style
   bread
8 eggs
Salt and pepper

Clean the mushrooms and cut them into slices. Toast them in a dry skillet on high heat for a couple of minutes. Add a generous pat of butter and sprinkle with thyme, salt, and pepper to taste.

Make two holes in each slice of bread, or one hole if the slices are not large enough for two eggs (approximately radius: 1½ to 2 inches/4 to 5 cm). Toast the slices in butter in a skillet on one side. Turn them over and crack the eggs into the holes. You can lift the slices to allow the egg to run out under the bread. The eggs are done when the whites are solid. Sprinkle with salt and pepper to taste. Serve with the toasted mushrooms.

BAKED BEANS WITH BACON & CHILI

This is a super easy and tasty breakfast food. You can easily make your baked beans ahead of time from scratch, but hey, you are welcome to cheat, especially if you would otherwise not make this dish! Buy the baked beans in a tin and taste your way to a perfect breakfast. If there are no children present, you can easily add 4 additional chilis to the dish. This will help your body wake up!

// INGREDIENTS

1 yellow onion

2 cloves garlic

Olive oil for frying

1¼ cups baked beans

2 teaspoons brown sugar

1–2 mild chilis

1 teaspoon smoked
   paprika

7 ounces (200 g) bacon

4 eggs

Salt and pepper

Chop the onion and mince the garlic. Let the onion and the garlic sweat in a pot with a lid in a little olive oil for a couple of minutes. Add the baked beans and the brown sugar, along with the chilis and the smoked paprika. Let the dish simmer for 15 to 20 minutes on a grate over the embers.

Fry the bacon in a skillet and serve the bacon with the chili and a cup of coffee.

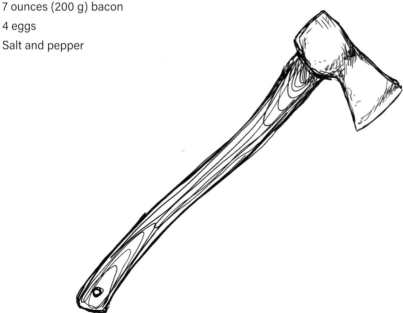

TOAST WITH SPINACH, BLUE CHEESE, MUSHROOMS & BACON

I love blue cheese cooked over a fire! To make the dish more kid-friendly you can substitute the blue cheese with a milder cheese of your choice. The smell and taste of mushrooms, blue cheese, and bacon is fantastic! And don't forget to make coffee as well.

// INGREDIENTS

4 slices of white French-style bread

Butter for frying

8 slices of bacon

3 portobello mushrooms

3.5 ounces (100 g) fresh spinach

4 slices blue cheese (or white cheddar if you prefer)

Salt and pepper to taste

Toast the bread in a skillet in some butter and move it to the side.

Fry the bacon in the same pan and move it to the side.

Clean the mushrooms, cut them into slices, and fry them in the bacon fat.

When the mushrooms are almost done, add the spinach with a generous pat of butter. Add salt and pepper to taste.

Put the warm mushroom and spinach mixture on top of the bread, then place the cheese and bacon on top.

TORTILLA ESPAÑOLA WITH CHORIZO & LEEKS

I'm crazy about this Spanish egg dish made on a campfire. I can eat the tortilla (which is the Spanish version of a frittata) for breakfast or dinner. Truthfully, I can eat it any time. You can easily change this recipe by using any leftovers that you may have. If you have potatoes, grilled meat, or vegetables from the day before, then just add them to the eggs.

// INGREDIENTS

4 slices bacon, finely
   chopped
5 slices chorizo, diced
2 yellow onions
1 clove garlic
4–5 boiled potatoes
   (approximately 1 pound/
   400 g)
8 eggs
½ teaspoon smoked paprika
½ bunch of parsley, coarsely
   chopped
½ teaspoon salt
¼ teaspoon freshly ground
   pepper
Olive oil for frying

Topping
Fresh thyme

Fry the bacon until it's crispy and let it drain. Let the chorizo sweat in the skillet until it gets some color and then put it to the side. Chop the onion and garlic finely, and brown both in the bacon fat. Cut the potatoes into quarters. Crack the eggs into a bowl and combine all the other ingredients with the eggs and mix well.

Put the skillet on a grate, which should be approximately 12 inches (30 cm) above the embers, and add the olive oil to the skillet. When the skillet is warm, pour the egg mixture into it and cover it with a lid or with a plate if you don't have a lid.

Cook the tortilla for approximately 10 to 15 minutes on each side, depending on the heat from the fire. Keep an eye on the skillet so that the bottom of the tortilla doesn't get burned. When the egg mixture is solid, you flip the tortilla so that it lies on the lid. Then carefully return it to the pan and continue cooking until it's ready. Top the tortilla with fresh thyme.

Suggestions for extra fillings: cabbage, scallions, mushrooms, etc.

The tortilla can also be served as a snack.

LUNCH

COWBOY TOAST WITH CHEDDAR, BLUE CHEESE, RED ONION & BBQ SAUCE

Panini presses and grilled cheese makers are ingenious inventions, and if you have one of these it's very easy to make the most delicious grilled sandwiches. Set up a table with the fixings so that both kids and adults can make their own favorite sandwiches. This is the world's best cowboy toast. I start by grilling the meat for a short time to make the patties deliciously crusty and smoky before they are assembled by the guests.

// INGREDIENTS

1 pound (500 g) hamburger beef

8 slices of French-style bread

4 slices cheddar cheese

4 slices blue cheese (can be omitted)

12 thin slices pickled red onion or raw red onion (see recipe for pickled red onions on page 174)

BBQ sauce

Oil for frying

Butter for frying

Salt and pepper

Add some oil to your panini press/grilled cheese maker and heat it over the campfire. Make sure the oil is evenly distributed on the surface. If you don't have one, you can use a skillet or place the bread directly on a grate.

Make 4 beef patties by hand and sprinkle with salt and pepper to taste. Grill the beef patties over the embers for 1 minute on each side to give them a nice crunchy surface.

Place the patties on the bread and then add a slice of cheddar cheese, a slice of blue cheese, 3 slices of red onion, and 2 teaspoons BBQ sauce on top. Cover with another slice of bread.

Melt 1 teaspoon butter in the panini press/toaster or in the skillet and grill the sandwiches over the embers. Turn them at regular intervals until they are crispy.

Tip: Remember that the panini press/toaster gets **very hot**, and so please use a piece of wood as a trivet to avoid burning the table. We usually yell: *"TOAST COMING!"* so that everyone knows that they need to be alert when the chef proudly walks up with the smoking hot sandwiches.

GRILLED HAM & CHEESE SANDWICHES

This is a recipe for a classic grilled ham and cheese sandwich. So easy and delicious! You can easily make the sandwiches at home and just warm them up by toasting them quickly on the campfire to save time. I love pickled red onion on food cooked over an open fire. It gives both a sweet and sour taste to the food.

// INGREDIENTS

8 slices French-style
   white bread
4 slices ham
8 slices white cheddar
   cheese
12 thin slices of pickled
   red onion (see
   recipe on page 174)
   or raw red onion
Oil for frying
Butter for frying
Salt and pepper

Add some oil to your panini press/grilled cheese maker and heat it over the campfire. If you don't have a stovetop panini press or grilled cheese maker, you can easily toast your bread in a regular skillet or on top of a grate.

Place 1 slice of ham, 2 slices of cheddar cheese, and 3 slices of pickled red onion or raw red onion on top of the bread and add salt and pepper to taste. Place another slice of bread on top.

Put 1 teaspoon butter into your skillet or toaster iron and toast your sandwiches over the embers. If you like, turn them over until the bread is slightly crispy.

HOT DOGS WITH HERB MAYO, PICKLED RED ONIONS & PANCETTA

Hot dogs never go out of fashion, and it's always great to roast them over a campfire. Prepare the toppings at home so that you only need to deal with the hot dogs and buns when you're outside. I like it when the hot dogs and the buns are a little burned so that they get that smoky flavor. Test your way to making the perfect hot dog and topping for you.

// INGREDIENTS

3.5 ounces pancetta or cooked strip of bacon
8 good quality hot dogs
8 brioche hot dog buns
Ketchup
Whole grain mustard
Herb mayo (see recipe below)
Picked red onions (see recipe on page 174)
Watercress or sorrel (optional)

¾ cup mayonnaise
1 tablespoon finely chopped chives (or other herbs)
¼ teaspoon lemon zest
Salt and pepper

Chop the pancetta or bacon for the topping.

Place the hot dogs on a grate until they are crispy and taste smoky. Slash the tops of the buns lengthwise and grill them until they are crispy.

Add the ketchup, mustard, herb mayo, pickled red onion, and chopped bacon on top. If you happen to have watercress or sorrel on hand, add it for an extra kick.

HERB MAYO

Mix some store-bought mayo with finely chopped chives and lemon zest and add salt and pepper to taste. The mayo should be a little acidic, so feel free to add some juice from the lemon if needed.

WAFFLES WITH SMOKED CHEESE, SALMON, SPINACH & RADISHES

The taste of waffles grilled over a fire is fantastic. The buttermilk gives them nice acidity, which goes well with the smoked salmon and smoked cheese.

// INGREDIENTS

2 handfuls fresh spinach

2 eggs

¾ cup (100 g) flour

2 tablespoons (30 g) melted butter

⅔ cup buttermilk

½ teaspoon salt

¼ teaspoon freshly ground black pepper

Sunflower oil and butter for frying

Toppings

4 slices cold smoked salmon

Smoked cheese

2 radishes

Watercress

Rinse the spinach and let it sweat in a skillet with a generous pat of butter. Let the moisture evaporate from the spinach, and then take it out of the skillet and chop it. Combine the eggs with the flour, melted butter, buttermilk, chopped spinach, and salt and pepper until the mixture is smooth.

Add 1 tablespoon sunflower oil to the waffle iron and heat it over the embers. Turn the waffle iron to make sure that the oil is evenly spread over both sides of the iron. This is very important to avoid burning the waffles. When the waffle iron is hot (this takes approximately 10 to 15 minutes), add a generous pat of butter to the iron. Then pour the batter into the iron and bake the waffles over the embers until they are crispy and golden. Keep turning the waffle iron and open it periodically to make sure that you don't burn the waffles.

Serve the spinach waffles with smoked salmon, smoked cheese, thinly sliced radishes, and watercress.

SMOKED CHEESE MIX

2 ounces (approximately 50 g) smoked cheese

2 ounces (50 g) crème fraîche

Salt and pepper

Lemon juice

Combine the smoked cheese with the crème fraîche and add salt and pepper to taste, and a few drops of lemon juice.

Tip: The waffle iron is very heavy; it works well to place it on top of a grate over the embers. Be careful not to drop it.

Tip: To make things easier when you're outdoors, make the waffle batter and the smoked cheese mix at home and transport the batter in a bottle and the cheese mix in a container.

GRILLED TROUT WITH HERBS & LEMON

The easiest food to cook on a campfire is a whole fish. Just fill a trout with herbs and butter before grilling. It'll end up tasting deliciously of smoke and fire. Try different herbs and vegetables if you like.

// INGREDIENTS

4 cleaned whole trout

Fresh dill

Fresh thyme

1 finely sliced red onion

2 lemons, sliced

4 tablespoons (60 g)
    butter, sliced

Salt and pepper

String for tying the fish

Dry the trout with paper towel and sprinkle salt and pepper on top of and inside it. Rinse the herbs and dry them before chopping them coarsely. Place the herbs, red onion, lemon slices, and the sliced butter inside the fish belly. Sprinkle with salt and pepper and if you like, tie the fish with string to keep the filling well inside the fish. Put the fish on a grate or grill over the embers and grill for 8 to 12 minutes on each side.

POTATOES IN SALT DOUGH SERVED WITH HERB CRÈME FRAÎCHE

Salt dough is fantastic to use when cooking meat, fish, or vegetables. It functions as a tailor-made frying pan that keeps in the juices and the flavors of what you're cooking. You don't eat the salt dough, as it becomes very hard and crusty after cooking. In this recipe, I'm using the salt dough as a vessel for making baked potatoes, which I'll serve with crème fraîche, herbs, and salt. I usually make some extra potatoes because there's a chance that some of them will burn.

// INGREDIENTS

6 washed potatoes
Flaky sea salt

Salt dough
4½ cups (600 g) flour
2⅛ cups (600 g) salt
Water

Herb crème fraîche
¾ cup crème fraîche
½ finely sliced red onion
2 tablespoons finely
    chopped leek
1 radish, finely chopped
½ teaspoon lemon juice
½ teaspoon salt

Build your fire and wait until you have good embers before you cook the potatoes. This will take about 2 hours.

Mix all the ingredients for the herb crème fraîche and let it cool in the fridge for 30 minutes.

Combine the flour and salt for the salt dough. Add the water a little at a time and knead. The dough should be firm and smooth and have the same consistency as playdough. Not too wet, not too dry. Add some flour if it's too wet, or a little water if it's too hard. Roll out the salt dough on parchment paper. The dough should be a little less than ¼-inch (½ cm) thick. Then pack the potatoes one at a time in a rectangle of salt dough making sure that the potatoes are completely enclosed. The salt from the dough will penetrate the potatoes.

Place salt dough packets directly on top of the embers. Turn the dough packets regularly and bake for approximately 40 to 45 minutes. To check for readiness, feel free to take out one potato, crack open the dough, and taste the potato.

Crack open the slightly cooled dough packets and serve the potatoes with the herb crème fraîche and a little flaky salt.

Tip: You can make the herb crème fraîche and the salt dough at home and pack the potatoes in the dough ahead of time.

Tip: You can also serve the potatoes as a side for a main course.

*Baked potatoes in salt dough.
Note that the crust of the salt
dough will burn.*

SNACKS

SALTED ALMONDS

Salted almonds are an easy-to-make delicious snack and a great addition to a campfire salad.

// INGREDIENTS

1¾ cups (200 g) whole almonds

¾ cups water

3 tablespoons sea salt

Bring salt and water to a boil in a skillet and add the almonds. Cook them at high heat while stirring until the water has evaporated. Make sure that the almonds don't burn, and that the salt attaches to the almonds. Turn the almonds onto a plate and let them cool.

POPCORN WITH SEA SALT & SMOKED PAPRIKA

Making popcorn over a campfire never goes out of fashion. The smell and taste are divine. You can make them in a pot or in a campfire popcorn popper. If you make them in a popcorn popper, make sure you hold them over the embers and not over the flames to avoid the popcorn burning.

// INGREDIENTS

1 cup popcorn kernels

3 tablespoons oil

Sea salt

½ teaspoon smoked
    paprika (optional)

Put the oil into a pot together with 3 popcorn kernels and place the pot over a grate over the embers. When the kernels pop, then the oil is hot enough. Add the rest of the popcorn kernels and put the lid on. When the popping subsides, remove the pot from the embers. Sprinkle the popcorn with sea salt or smoked paprika if you like.

DATES WITH CHILI & BACON

The sweetness from the dates, the crispy bacon, and just a little bit of chili makes this snack truly delicious. If you like you can try to roll the bacon around vegetables, e.g., asparagus.

// INGREDIENTS

2 mild chilis
14 pitted dates
14 bacon strips
Olive oil for frying

Rinse the chilis and cut them in thin strips lengthwise. Place 1 to 2 chili strips on top of each date and roll the bacon around the date. You can use a toothpick or a skewer to hold the bacon in place. Toast the dates on a grate or in a skillet over the embers until the bacon is nice and crispy.

This is perhaps not the most elegant of snacks, but the taste is fantastic.

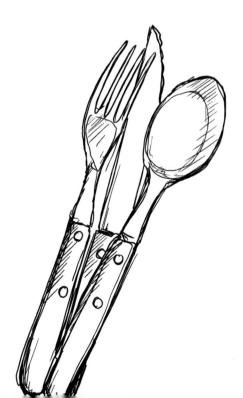

BREAD ON A STICK WITH SUN-DRIED TOMATOES & PARMESAN CHEESE

Campfire bread on a stick is a classic, but you need to be patient to make it both crispy on the outside and baked through. Far too often you see campfire bread that is black on the outside and completely uncooked on the inside. We have busy lives, and we like to do everything fast. It's a great joy to cook the perfect campfire bread on a stick. Remember that it needs to be made slowly over embers, not over flames. Here are a couple of variations of bread on a stick which can be enjoyed by itself, or along with a meal. If you can't find fresh yeast, you can use about 3 teaspoons active dry yeast instead. Just make sure the milk is warm (but not hot) to activate the yeast properly.

// INGREDIENTS

½ cup (40 g) butter

1¼ cups milk

1 ounce (30 g) fresh yeast
   (or see note above about
   active dry yeast substitute)

1 teaspoon sugar

2 teaspoons salt

10 chopped sun-dried
   tomatoes

1.7 ounces (50 g) diced
   parmesan cheese

4 cups (500 g) flour

Melt the butter in a pot or skillet and add the milk. Pour the mixture into a bowl and add the fresh yeast. Add sugar, salt, chopped sun-dried tomatoes, parmesan cheese, and flour, and knead the dough well. Cover it with a dish towel and let the dough rise for 30 to 60 minutes.

Take a piece of the dough and roll it into a thin "sausage" and then skewer it on a stick with the bark removed. Cook the bread slowly over the embers until it's nice and crispy.

PIZZA ON A STICK WITH PEPPERONI, MOZZARELLA & RED ONION

It's great fun to make pizza on a stick over a campfire. Set up a workstation where kids and grownups can select their favorite pizza toppings. Make sure that you don't overstuff the pizza. It can be hard to do especially when you're hungry, but it's better to make many small pizzas than one big one. If you can't find fresh yeast, you can use about 3 teaspoons active dry yeast instead. Just make sure the water is warm (but not hot) to activate the yeast properly.

// INGREDIENTS

1 ounce (30 g) fresh yeast
(or see note above
about active dry yeast
substitute)

1 cup water

1 teaspoon honey

2 teaspoons salt

3¼ cups (400 g) flour

Fillings

Pizza sauce

4 ounces shredded
mozzarella

1 red onion, thinly sliced

8–10 slices of pepperoni or
chorizo

1 teaspoon oregano

Mix the yeast with water, honey, and salt in a bowl. Add almost all the flour and knead the dough well. Add more flour if the dough is sticky. Cover with a dish towel and let it rise for one hour.

Look for a few sticks that can be used for making the pizza and remove the bark from approximately 6 inches of each stick.

Divide the dough into 8 to 10 servings and use a rolling pin to shape them into rectangles. Add a little bit of pizza sauce on top, followed by the mozzarella, red onion, and pepperoni, and sprinkle with oregano. Don't add too much filling. Roll the pizza rectangles lengthwise into thin "sausages" and then skewer them on the sticks and slowly cook them over the embers until they are crispy and golden. They should taste a little burnt.

Pizza on a stick with pepperoni, mozzarella & red onion, page 80

Cinnamon buns on a stick, page 152

Bread on a stick with sun-dried tomatoes & parmesan cheese, page 79

STARTERS

POTATO AND LEEK SOUP WITH BACON & FRIED POTATO STICKS

Soups are easy to make on a campfire. You simply cut up the vegetables, put them into a pot with some stock, and simmer them for as long as you like. This soup is my youngest son's favorite, and he makes it often. It's easy to make and it's delicious. You can make it extra rustic by leaving the peels on the potatoes.

// INGREDIENTS

4 leeks cut in half
    lengthwise and sliced
    (use only the white part)
1 finely sliced onion
1½ tablespoons (20 g) butter
5 potatoes, finely diced
1 parsnip, finely diced
1 quart chicken or vegetable
    stock
⅓–½ cup white wine
½–1 cup whipping cream
Salt and pepper

Topping
Bacon, chopped
Chives, finely chopped
Fried potato sticks (see
    recipe on the next page)

Melt the butter in a pot placed over the fire and add the leeks and onion to sweat in the pot for a couple of minutes. Add the potatoes and the parsnip and give the vegetables another couple of minutes before adding the stock and the white wine. Let the soup simmer for approximately 30 minutes. Add the cream to taste, heat up the soup, and season with salt and pepper.

Serve the warm potato and leek soup with crispy bacon on top, finely chopped chives, and fried potato sticks.

Tip: It's important to have the ingredients prepped and ready to go before you start cooking the soup.

Tip: It's a good idea to add a little extra oil to the pot when you fry the vegetables to make sure that they don't burn.

Continued on the next page ▶

FRIED POTATO STICKS

2 large potatoes
Oil for frying
Salt

Fry the potatoes at home. First cut them into the size of matchsticks and place them in a bowl with cold water to remove excess starches. You could use a mandoline to slice them, or a food processor with the right attachment, or use a handheld grater. Remove the potatoes from the water and dry them well with a clean kitchen towel. Fry the potato sticks in a skillet or pot in warm oil until they are crispy and brown. Place the cooked potato sticks on paper towel and sprinkle them with salt.

SUMMER SOUP WITH ROOT VEGETABLES & HERBS

This Summer Soup is loveliness in a pot with delicious herbs. It's easy to make, and you can use your own favorite herbs or vegetables or fresh shoots as ingredients. If you would like the soup to taste extra smoky, you can roast the vegetables on a grate over the fire before putting them into the pot.

// INGREDIENTS

2 coarsely chopped
    yellow onions

2 finely chopped cloves
    of garlic

½ sliced fennel

4 parsnips, sliced

4 carrots, sliced

1 leek, sliced

4 potatoes, diced

½ bunch parsley

½ bunch dill

Olive oil for frying

1 quart chicken stock

Salt and pepper

Let the onion, garlic, and fennel sweat in oil until everything is lightly browned. Add the the rest of the vegetables and the stock and let the soup simmer for 30 minutes or more. Add salt and pepper to taste.

Tip: If there are other vegetables or herbs that you feel like adding, go ahead.

STEAMED BLUE MUSSELS IN WHITE WINE WITH CREAM & ITALIAN PARSLEY

This is one of my favorite dishes. There's nothing nicer than to sit together and enjoy mussels made on a campfire. Serve the mussels in a bowl and use the shells as spoons for opening the mussels. Toast some good bread that you can dip into the delicious mussel broth and note that a glass of nice chilled white wine with the mussels is a must for the gourmet in nature.

// INGREDIENTS

4½ pounds (2 kg) blue
    mussels
Olive oil for frying
1 red onion, finely
    chopped
2 cloves garlic, minced
1 mild chili
5 sprigs fresh thyme
1 cup white wine
1 cup heavy cream
Salt and pepper

Garnish
Chopped Italian parsley

For serving
Bread
Aioli or chili mayo

Start by cleaning the mussels thoroughly in a large bowl of cold water and cutting the "beard" from the mussels. All the mussels that are broken or that don't open after 2 minutes need to be discarded. If you're in doubt whether to keep them or not, then throw them out to be on the safe side. Place the cleaned mussels in a colander to drain.

Heat the oil in a pot and let the onion, garlic, chili, and the fresh thyme sweat for a couple of minutes. Add the white wine and heat the broth before you add the mussels. The mussels should steam for approximately 5 minutes in the pot with a lid. Shake the pan a couple of times and add salt and pepper to taste. Add the heavy cream to make a creamy and delicious mussel broth.

Place the cooked mussels in a large bowl and sprinkle with finely chopped parsley. If you see any mussels that haven't opened, then discard them immediately.

Serve with bread, aioli or chili mayo, and chilled white wine.

Tip: It's important that the mussels are transported in a cool bag surrounded by ice packs or in bag with ice from your fishmonger, and that they are kept cool until you are ready to use them. They should be eaten immediately after they are cooked.

JUMBO SHRIMP WITH CHILI, GARLIC, CORIANDER & LIME

The aroma of grilled shrimp and garlic is hard to beat. This is appetizer is both easy and super delicious. When grilling the shrimp, it's important to make sure that the embers are hot and glowing.

// INGREDIENTS

1 pound (approximately 400 g) jumbo shrimp—tail on, peeled and deveined

3½ tablespoons (50 g) butter

1 teaspoon smoked paprika

1 mild red chili, finely chopped

½ yellow onion, finely chopped

2 cloves garlic, finely minced

¾ inch (2 cm) fresh ginger, finely minced

1 lime

Melt the butter in a skillet over the embers. Add the smoked paprika, chili, onion, garlic, and ginger, and let everything sweat for couple of minutes. Drain the prawns in a colander and dry them with some kitchen towel. Place them in the skillet and fry them for 2 to 3 minutes.

Serve with lime and fresh coriander or parsley.

GRILLED CABBAGE WITH SESAME SEEDS, TERIYAKI & RED ONION

I'm crazy about fresh red and green pointed cabbage. Pointed cabbages are more elegant than white cabbage and taste divine when grilled on a campfire, but if you can't find them, feel free to use white cabbage instead. You can grill them whole or cut them into quarters or chop them finely and roast them in a skillet. If you cook them in a hot skillet, they will get a smoky and slightly burned taste. If you decide to grill them whole, they need to cook for 40 minutes and be turned regularly. When the cabbages are done, you need to remove the outer layer before eating them. Yum!

// INGREDIENTS

1 red onion
1 red or green pointed
      cabbage (or white
      cabbage)
Olive oil
1 head romaine lettuce
Teriyaki sauce
1 tablespoon toasted
      sesame seeds
Salt and pepper

Grill the red onion unpeeled over the embers for 20 to 30 minutes. Turn it at regular intervals.

Rinse the cabbage and cut it into quarters. Pour a little olive oil into the skillet, add the cabbage, and let cook at high heat making sure that it burns slightly to give it the smoky taste that we want. Let it cool.

Rinse the romaine lettuce and pat it dry with a kitchen towel. Arrange the leaves on a plate or in a bowl.

Remove the peel from the onion. Cut the grilled onions and the cabbage and place them on top of the lettuce. Pour some olive oil and teriyaki sauce over the salad, and sprinkle with the toasted sesame seeds. Add salt and freshly milled pepper to taste.

Tip: The sesame seeds can be substituted with toasted hazelnuts or pine nuts. Alternatively, you can top the salad with pea shoots or other greens.

GRILLED HOKKAIDO PUMPKIN WITH GOAT CHEESE & HONEY

Goat cheese and Hokkaido pumpkin (or similar squashes) is a fantastic combination. Grill the pumpkin over a hot skillet until it gets a little charred.

// INGREDIENTS

1 Hokkaido pumpkin
(or similar edible
squash)
Goat cheese log
2 tablespoons olive oil
for frying
Fresh thyme
Acacia honey
Flaky salt and pepper

Cut the pumpkin lengthwise into slices and remove the seeds. Cut off the skin. Cut the goat cheese log into slices that are just under ¼-inch (½ cm) wide. Heat a skillet, add the olive oil, place the skillet over the embers, and sauté the pumpkin for 2 to 3 minutes on one side. It's OK if it's slightly burned. Turn over the pumpkin slices and top with slices of goat cheese and fresh thyme. Sauté for another 2 to 3 minutes until the cheese is melting.

Sprinkle the pumpkin and cheese with flaky salt and pepper and drip some honey over the finished dish.

Tip: You can use plain pumpkin for this dish. Bigger slices can be grilled directly on a grate.

GRILLED SALAD WITH FENNEL, GREEN CABBAGE & TOASTED PUMPKIN SEEDS

When you cook over a campfire, you must be able to taste that the food has been cooked over fire. Otherwise, you might as well cook the food at home. I love grilled salads and charred vegetables. Peppers and red onion turn wonderfully sweet when grilled, and green cabbage becomes crispy with a slight bitterness when it's cooked over high heat.

// INGREDIENTS

1 red pepper

1 yellow pepper

3 scallions

1 leek

½ fennel

6 green cabbage leaves

1 red apple, diced

Toasted pumpkin seeds

Chopped salted
    almonds (see recipe
    on page 73)

Balsamic vinegar

Salt and pepper

Wash and rinse all the vegetables. Cut the tops of the peppers and remove the seeds. Cut the stems of the scallions and the leek. Cut the fennel in quarters lengthwise. Cook all the vegetables over high heat on a grate over the embers, so that they get nicely charred. Use long grill tongs and fireproof gloves to avoid burning yourself. The vegetable leaves become nice and crispy resembling chips and can be enjoyed as a snack.

When the vegetables are ready, take them off the fire to cool. Cut the grilled vegetables into smaller pieces and make a salad with the diced apple, the toasted pumpkin seeds, and the chopped salted almonds. Add salt, pepper, and balsamic to the salad just before serving.

Tip: Substitute some of the vegetables with your own favorite vegetables such as fresh onions instead of green cabbage.

BAKED RED ONION WITH BUTTER, THYME & FLAKY SALT

This is a small and delicious dish by itself, or it can be a side dish for a main course. Perfectly grilled red onions are sweet, soft, and slightly burnt and crispy on the outside. With melted butter and a sprinkling of flaky salt on top these onions are hard to beat. It's a good idea to make some extras just in case a couple of them get too burnt.

// INGREDIENTS

6 red onions
¼ cup (50 g) butter
Fresh thyme
Flaky sea salt

The onions should not be peeled but the tops should be cut off. Cut off a little of the bottom as well so that the onions can stand on their own. Make a cross with a knife at the top of the onions, so that they open when you bake them.

Push the embers from one side of the campfire to the middle. Place the onions standing up where the embers were before they were moved. Bake them for 30 to 40 minutes and turn them periodically.

Serve with a generous pat of butter, fresh thyme, and flaky salt.

RUSTIC SKEWERS WITH PORK, CABBAGE & MUSHROOMS

These are the world's most delicious and most rustic grill skewers. When I run cooking courses, I ask the participants to go out and find a stick that they can carve to be used as a skewer. Looking for skewers helps everyone to feel present in nature.

// INGREDIENTS

½ pound (200 g) pork neck chops cut into ¾-inch (2 cm) cubes

Teriyaki sauce

1 red onion, cut in quarters

Green cabbage, cut into small cubes

Bacon, cut into squares

10 mushrooms, washed and cut in quarters

Sesame seeds

Look for 12- to 16-inch long sticks that can be used for grilling skewers. The tip of each skewer should be just under ¼-inch in diameter; if the sticks are too thick, the mushrooms will fall off.

Pour the teriyaki sauce over the meat and then start placing the food on the skewers.
I follow this order: meat, red onion, green cabbage, bacon, mushrooms, and then I repeat the same once more. But they are your skewers, so you decide the order.

Grill the skewers over high heat until they get nicely charred and smoky, approximately 2 minutes on each side. Make sure that the meat is cooked through. Approximately 20 seconds before the skewers are ready, sprinkle them with sesame seeds so that they will have time to be nicely toasted.

MAINS

EGG WRAPS WITH SALAD, BACON, SHREDDED CHEESE & CRÈME FRAÎCHE DRESSING

Egg wraps are thin omelets that are delicious and easy to make on a campfire. If you would like your wrap to have a smokier taste, then you can grill the vegetables on a grate over the campfire first. It's useful to have a knife handy in case you decide to cut the wraps in half.

// INGREDIENTS

8 eggs

1 head romaine lettuce,
    rinsed and sliced

1 tomato, sliced

1 cucumber, cut in strips

½ head of cabbage

½ red onion, sliced

3.5 ounces (100 g) grated
    cheese

8 slices fried bacon

Oil for frying

Salt and pepper

Crème fraîche dressing

¾ cup crème fraîche

1–2 cloves garlic, pressed

½ teaspoon lemon juice

1 pinch of salt

1 pinch of pepper

Combine all the ingredients for the crème fraîche dressing, and let it cool in the fridge for 20 minutes.

Add some olive oil to a skillet and place it over the embers to warm up. Crack two eggs into a bowl and add salt and pepper and whisk the eggs with a fork. Add the mixture to the skillet and turn it to make sure that the egg mixture spreads out evenly. Cook the wrap for approximately 1 to 3 minutes per side. Carefully remove the wrap by placing a palette knife under the wrap, then flip it over without breaking it. Make all the 4 wraps this way.

Make a salad with the romaine lettuce, tomato, cucumber, cabbage, and red onion.

Place the salad on top of one half of the wrap. Add cheese, the crème fraîche dressing, and bacon, and close the wrap carefully.

Tip: Make your own favorite salad and use other meats if you like. Alternatively, you can make a meatless wrap.

CEVAPCICI WITH BELL PEPPERS & HAYDARI DIP

Balkan rolls, or cevapcici, made over the campfire taste amazingly good, and they make all ages happy. These rolled meat patties are made with ground beef and lamb, and everyone knows that lamb roasted over a fire is simply divine. When you're ready for grilling, drip the soy and garlic marinade into the fire so that the infused flames kiss the meat. The aroma of smoke, campfire, and the meat is simply terrific. Feel free to double the recipe. The cevapcici rolls are served with grilled bell peppers filled with haydari, a Turkish dip that can be made with feta cheese, ajvar, chilis, olive oil, parsley, and garlic. It's a delicious addition to the campfire menu.

// INGREDIENTS

¾ pound (300 g) ground beef

½ pound (200 g) ground lamb

½ teaspoon smoked paprika

1 teaspoon salt

1 pinch freshly ground black pepper

1–2 cloves garlic, finely minced

Approximately ¼ cup water

Olive oil for frying

Marinade

½ cup soy sauce

½ cup olive oil

1 clove garlic, finely minced

5–10 drops Tabasco sauce

Salt and pepper to taste

Mix the ground meats with the spices, garlic, and water. Let it rest for 30 minutes if you can. Meanwhile, make the marinade.

Shape the ground meat mixture into small oblong sausage shapes and swirl them around in the marinade. If you like, leave them to soak in the marinade for a little while. Grill the cevapcici at high heat to give them a crispy coating all around. The marinade will drip down into the fire and the flames will infuse the meat with flavor.

Serve the delicious cevapcici with grilled long bell peppers filled with haydari (see next page).

Tip: If you can't get hold of ground lamb, then you can use all ground beef instead.

Continued on the next page ▶

GRILLED SNACKING PEPPERS FILLED WITH HAYDARI DIP

1 long Italian-style sweet
    pepper per person
½–¾ cup (100–200 g)
    creamed haydari dip or
    herbed cheese spread

Rinse the sweet peppers, cut the tops off, and remove the seeds. Fill them with haydari dip or cheese spread and grill the peppers on a grate over the embers.

Tip: You can buy haydari dip in Turkish or Middle Eastern food stores.

SANDWICH WITH CRISPY PORK, APPLE & TANGY MAYO

This sandwich is inspired by the award-winning porchetta burger that I made at the NorthSide festival in Denmark. I have chosen a slightly easier version here. Grilled pork on a campfire is delicious, and the crispy pork rinds together with the rest of the filling will be a showstopper at your campfire.

// INGREDIENTS

4 pork neck chops

4 ciabatta-style rolls

Tangy mayo (see recipe on the next page)

1 apple, sliced

½ red or green pointed cabbage (or regular red cabbage)

Coarse ground mustard

10 small, pickled cucumbers

1 pickled red onion (see recipe on page 174)

1 handful of crispy pork rinds

Salt and pepper

Rinse the cabbage and cut it lengthwise and cut off the bottom. Cut it in half.

Sprinkle the pork neck chops with salt and pepper and grill them on a grate over embers for 2 to 4 minutes on each side based on the thickness of the chops and the heat from the fire. If you are in doubt about how long to cook the meat, you can cut off a piece to check that it's cooked through.

Cut the ciabatta-style rolls and toast them lightly over the embers until they are crispy. I like mine to be a little charred.

You can either fill the sandwiches for your guests or place the toppings on a table and let the guests make their own sandwiches.

Add the tangy mayo to the bottom part of the roll, followed by the grilled pork meat, 1 to 2 apple slices, a handful of cabbage, coarse ground mustard to taste, pickled cucumbers, red onion, and 4 to 5 crispy pork rinds. Add a good spoonful of mayo on top and close the sandwich.

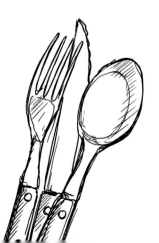

Continued on the next page ▶

TANGY MAYO

1 cup mayonnaise

½–1 teaspoon lemon
    juice

¼ teaspoon salt and a
    sprinkling of freshly
    ground black pepper

Mix the mayonnaise with the lemon juice, salt, and pepper. It should taste tangy, so don't hold back with the lemon juice.

Tip: Garnish with pea shoots or other fresh herbs, if desired.

Tip: Use coffee filters like paper wraps or pockets to hold the sandwiches.

RACK OF LAMB & RED CABBAGE TZATZIKI WITH MINT

I love lamb cooked over a campfire. If you want to treat your guests to something really special, cook these "lamb lollipops" for them. Smoky grilled lamb with garlic is delicious, and the cabbage tzatziki goes perfectly with this dish. I like to grill a couple of cabbage leaves before I mix them into the tzatziki to make the dish extra smoky.

// INGREDIENTS

1 crown of lamb or
    4 lamb chops
3½ tablespoons olive
    oil
1 clove garlic, minced
2 sprigs fresh rosemary
½ teaspoon salt
1 pinch black pepper

Cut the crown of lamb into single chops and trim off any extra fat and membranes from the bones. Make a marinade of olive oil, garlic, rosemary, salt, and pepper, and leave the meat to rest in the marinade for at least 30 minutes.

Grill the lamb over high heat on a grate over the embers about 2 minutes on each side, until the surface of the meat is crispy and the inside is pink. If in doubt, cut into the meat to check for doneness.

RED CABBAGE TZATZIKI

½ red pointed cabbage
    (or regular red
    cabbage)
½ cup crème fraîche
2 cloves garlic, minced
10 leaves fresh mint,
    chopped
¼ teaspoon ground
    cumin
½ teaspoon lemon juice
Salt and pepper

Rinse and cut the cabbage in half lengthwise and cut off the stem. Take two leaves off the cabbage, and finely slice the rest. Grill the two whole leaves until they are slightly burned. Let them cool, and then cut them finely and mix them in with the rest of the sliced cabbage.

Make a dressing of crème fraîche, garlic, chopped mint, cumin, lemon juice, and salt and pepper to taste. Combine the cabbage and the dressing. Add some more crème fraîche if you prefer a creamier texture.

JUICY BARBEQUED SPARERIBS WITH GRILLED COLESLAW

All cuts of meat with good marbling are perfect for campfire cooking, because the fat drips down into the fire and ignites the flames. This effect gives the meat extra TLC and a smoky taste. These thick spareribs are delicious when they get crispy, and they have a real authentic barbequed taste.

// INGREDIENTS

8 thick spareribs
1 cup barbeque sauce
Salt and pepper

Sprinkle the spareribs with salt and pepper and marinate them in the BBQ sauce. Grill the spareribs for 3 to 5 minutes on each side. Make sure that they are cooked through.

GRILLED COLESLAW

¼ white cabbage
2 carrots, washed and
    coarsely grated
½ cup crème fraîche
2 tablespoons mayonnaise
1 teaspoon mustard
½–1 teaspoon lemon juice
1–2 teaspoons sugar
½ teaspoon salt
1 pinch black pepper

Rinse the cabbage and divide it lengthwise in 4 parts. Cut off the stem. Remove two whole cabbage leaves and grill them on high heat until they are slightly charred, which gives the coleslaw a nice smoky taste. Let them cool and slice the cabbage finely. Combine with the grated carrots.

Make a dressing of crème fraîche, mayo, mustard, lemon juice, sugar, salt, and pepper. The dressing should have a sweet and sour taste. If you like, you can add more lemon juice or sugar, and finally combine all the ingredients and mix them evenly.

Toss the cabbage and the carrots in the dressing.

COQ AU VIN

For this recipe I use chicken thighs, but you can also use duck or pheasant meat. This is a delicious dish to simmer. If you can get fresh pearl onions, do it, but if not, jarred will work.

// INGREDIENTS

4 chicken legs

5 ounces (about 150 g) diced bacon

2 red onions in quarters

2 cloves of garlic, minced

15 pearl onions, peeled or from a jar

½ pound (250 g) cleaned mushrooms, cut in quarters

1 bunch chopped thyme

1 handful chopped parsley

3 bay leaves

2 cups chicken stock or bouillon

½ bottle red wine

Olive oil

Salt and pepper

Sauce

3½ tablespoons (50 g) chilled butter

2 tablespoons flour

½ cup water

For serving

Cooked rice

Sprinkle the chicken thighs with salt and pepper. Grill them on a grate over the embers for approximately 2 to 3 minutes on each side so that they get nice and crispy.

Add the diced bacon to a skillet and let it sweat for a short while. Remove it and put to the side. Then sweat the red onion, garlic, and pearl onions in the bacon fat for 2 minutes. If you like, add some olive oil if you think that more fat is needed. Add the chicken pieces, mushrooms, thyme, parsley, bay leaves, the diced bacon, the stock, and red wine. Let the dish simmer for 35 minutes or longer. Add salt and pepper to taste.

Remove the chicken legs with a slotted spoon and add the cold butter to the sauce and mix until it's smooth. Combine flour and water and add it to the sauce while stirring. If the sauce needs to be thicker, feel free to add a little more of the flour mixture. Add the chicken legs to the sauce and heat up the dish.

Serve with cooked rice.

Tip: If you would like the mushrooms to have a smoky taste you can grill them before cutting them into quarters.

LAMB STEW WITH POTATOES & ROSEMARY

Making stews on a campfire is easy and delicious. After you've cut the vegetables and added them to the pot, you can relax by the fire and enjoy a glass of beer. I like to add the potatoes to the stew so that they get the same taste as the other ingredients. Doing this means that you only need one pot. A win-win for the cook.

// INGREDIENTS

1¼ pounds (600 g) lamb
    meat (leg of lamb or
    chops), cut into cubes
3 onions, cut into quarters
5 cloves garlic, minced
4 parsnips, sliced
4 carrots, sliced
½ celery root (celeriac),
    diced
1 pound (500 g) washed
    unpeeled baby potatoes,
    halved
¼ teaspoon ground cumin
1–2 teaspoons smoked
    paprika
4¼ cups lamb or beef stock
1 bottle of dark beer
    (approximately
    1½ cups/330 ml)
1 sprig fresh rosemary
½–1 cup heavy cream
Olive oil for frying
Salt and pepper

Sweat the meat in olive oil in a pot for a short time and then remove the meat and put it to the side. Continue by letting the onion and garlic sweat in the olive oil for a couple of minutes and then add the rest of the vegetables, the potatoes, and the spices and let cook over low heat for 3 to 4 minutes. Add the meat, the stock, the beer, and the rosemary, and let the stew simmer for a minimum of 30 minutes. Add the heavy cream and heat the stew and finally add the salt and pepper to taste. When the potatoes are cooked through and the stew has the desired taste, it's ready to serve.

Tip: If you would like the broth to be thicker, make a paste of 2 tablespoons of flour with slightly less than ½ cup of water and add a little of the mixture to the stew. Let it boil until you reach the desired thickness.

TACOS WITH TWO KINDS OF MEAT

Enjoying food by the campfire with guests is a lot of fun. I love to grill meat and veggies and to prepare lots of toppings served in bowls to allow the guests to make their own perfect tacos. Who dares to add some extra jalapeños on their taco? You can use any kind of grilled meat or vegetables for your tacos. Test different ingredients until you find your favorite combinations.

// INGREDIENTS
4 chicken breasts

Olive oil for frying

Salt and pepper

12 soft corn tortillas

Toppings
2 heads lettuce, washed and
finely sliced

¾ cup ready-made salsa

Sweet chili sauce (store-
bought)

5 ounces grated cheddar
cheese

Pickled jalapeños or pickled
red onions (see recipe on
page 174)

½ cup crème fraîche

Fresh cilantro, washed and
coarsely chopped

The prepared toppings are placed in small bowls.

Pour a little olive oil on the chicken breasts and sprinkle them with salt and pepper. Grill the chicken on a grate over the embers for approximately 3 to 4 minutes on each side until they are crispy. Make sure that they are cooked through. If you are in doubt, cut into one of the chicken pieces to check for readiness.

Remove the cooked chicken breasts from the grate and cut them into thin slices. Toast the soft tacos or tortillas in a skillet or over a grate for 10 to 15 seconds on each side. When they are ready, you can pack them inside a clean dish towel to keep them soft and warm.

Place the chicken and the toppings on a table to allow the guests to make their own tacos with lettuce, chicken, salsa, grated cheese, sweet chili sauce, pickled jalapeños or red onions, and fresh cilantro.

SPICY GOULASH SOUP

This Spicy Goulash Soup warms you inside and is especially good in winter or on a chilly day. And it's easy to make!

// INGREDIENTS

1 pound (500 g) beef, sliced

5 ounces (150 g) bacon, diced

2 yellow onions, coarsely chopped

3 cloves garlic, minced

5 potatoes, diced

4 parsley roots, sliced (substitute with parsnip)

4 carrots, sliced

1 red bell pepper, finely sliced

1 mild chili, finely chopped

2 tablespoons paprika

1 teaspoon coarse salt

½ teaspoon cumin

2–3 bay leaves

8 whole black peppercorns

2 quarts beef stock

½ cup chopped tomatoes

½ cup (about 70 g) tomato puree

Olive oil for frying

Salt and freshly milled black pepper

Sides

Crème fraîche

Finely chopped parsley

Crusty bread and butter

You can easily prep for this dish at home. Chop and cut the vegetables, cut the meat into cubes, and fry the bacon. Place the meat, bacon, and the vegetables in individual containers. Onion and garlic should be prepared and packed separately.

Add the olive oil to a pot to heat, followed by the meat, and let it sweat in the oil.

Add the onion and garlic and let everything cook for 2 to 3 minutes. Add the spices, the rest of the vegetables, and the fried bacon. Give it a couple of minutes before adding the stock, the chopped tomatoes, and the tomato puree. If you can, let the soup simmer for at least 30 minutes, but the longer the better. Taste the soup and add salt and pepper if needed. The soup should be well spiced and have some heat, but not so much that it makes you sweat!

Serve the soup piping hot in soup bowls with a dollop of crème fraîche on top.

GRILLED PORK TENDERLOIN WITH HERB BUTTER

If you prepare the herb butter at home, then this delicious dish takes no time at all to cook. Crispy pork tenderloin with a little smoke flavor is simply fantastic and easy to make. You need some good embers and high heat to make the tenderloin crispy. When the meat is crispy, cut it into slices and finish it off on a campfire grill to achieve perfection.

// INGREDIENTS

2 pork tenderloins
Olive oil
Salt and pepper

For serving
Herb butter
Baked potatoes, or a
   grilled salad

Clean the tenderloins and cut off the membranes. Brush the meat with olive oil and grill both tenderloins at high heat in a skillet over embers. They should be well-browned before you cut the tenderloins into 1-inch (2½-cm) thick slices.

Then place the slices on a grill over the campfire at high heat to crisp them for approximately 1 to 2 minutes on each side. I like my tenderloins to be slightly pink on the inside. Sprinkle with salt and pepper.

Serve the tenderloin slices very warm with herb butter and baked potatoes or a grilled vegetable salad.

HERB BUTTER

10 tablespoons (150 g)
   butter, softened
1 clove garlic, minced
½ teaspoon salt
1 pinch black pepper

Combine all the ingredients and place the soft butter on a piece of waxed paper or parchment, then carefully roll it into a log with the help of the paper. Roll up the ends of the paper so that the butter will be shaped like a round log. Keep the herb butter in a cool place until you're ready to use it.

RIBEYE STEAK WITH BLUE CHEESE & GRILLED CABBAGE WITH PARMESAN CHEESE

Ribeye steak is one of my favorite cuts of beef. The marbling of the meat makes for an exquisite flavor when it's grilled over a campfire. If fat makes you worried, feel free to cut off any excess fat from the meat. The grilled ribeye steak with melted blue cheese produces a fantastic umami taste. If you don't like blue cheese, you can omit it. The steak works well on its own.

// INGREDIENTS

4 thick ribeye steaks
1 red pointed cabbage
   (or regular red or
   white cabbage)
Olive oil
Parmesan cheese,
   freshly grated
Salt and pepper
4 thin slices of blue
   cheese (can be
   omitted)

Sprinkle the steaks with salt and pepper.

Wash the cabbage and cut it in quarters lengthwise. Grill the cabbage pieces on a grate over embers for approximately 10 to 12 minutes. Remember to turn them regularly.

When you're ready to serve the cabbage quarters, drizzle them with some olive oil, a sprinkling of salt, pepper, and freshly grated Parmesan cheese.

Grill the steaks over embers for approximately 2 to 4 minutes, depending on how well-done you like your steak. When the steaks are ready on one side, turn them over, and place the blue cheese on top to allow the cheese to melt.

Serve the juicy steak with the grilled cabbage.

CAMPFIRE BURGER WITH BACON, CHEDDAR, BLUE CHEESE & BBQ SAUCE

A greasy burger is always a winner, but you can't beat a burger that's been cooked over a campfire with smoky grilled bacon and melted cheese on a toasted brioche bun. This burger is so good that it'll make you cry . . . or maybe that's the smoke in your eyes.

// INGREDIENTS

1 pound (approximately 500 g) ground beef

4 slices cheddar cheese

4 slices blue cheese

4 slices grilled bacon

5 brioche buns

Ketchup

5 leaves romaine lettuce

4 tomato slices

Pickles

Pickled red onion (see recipe on page 174) or sliced red onion

4 tablespoons prepared BBQ sauce

Salt and pepper

Make four round beef patties and sprinkle them with salt and pepper. Grill them approximately 3 to 4 minutes on each side so that they are slightly crispy on the outside but preferably a little pink inside. When you turn the patties, place one slice of cheddar cheese and 1 slice of blue cheese on top (make sure everyone likes blue cheese) followed by a slice of bacon.

Cut the brioche buns in half and toast them over the fire.

Add the ketchup on the bottom part of the bun and place the meat patty with the cheese and bacon on top. Follow up with the lettuce, tomato, pickles, pickled red onion, and finally a little barbeque sauce.

Tip: You can serve the burgers inside paper coffee filters to avoid any spillage.

CHILI CON CARNE

There is nothing better than spicy dishes that warm you right up when you're cooking outdoors in cool weather. I once made the world's largest pot of chili for a street food event where almost no one came, and I ended up with 176 pounds of chili con carne. I tried to sell it calling it "Mexican Lasagna," "Mexican meat sauce," "Mexican wraps," etc., until I realized that today's kids are perhaps not as crazy about chili con carne as I am. I just love this classic dish that works so well made on a campfire.

// INGREDIENTS

1 pound (500 g) beef, cut into
    chunks
4 tablespoons olive oil
2 yellow onions, cut in
    quarters
5 cloves garlic, minced
1 bottle dark beer
1 quart beef stock
3 tablespoons smoked paprika
½ teaspoon cayenne pepper
1 cinnamon stick
1 bunch fresh thyme
1 red bell pepper
1 green bell pepper
2 mild chilies
1 cup chopped tomatoes
4½ tablespoons (70 g) tomato
    paste
½ cup canned kidney beans
½ cup canned black beans
Salt and pepper

Toppings
Crème fraîche, lime,
finely chopped red onion,
    peanuts

Warm up the oil in a pot and add the meat; brown the meat well before removing it. Add the onion and garlic to sweat in the oil for a couple of minutes and return the meat to the pot. Add the beer, beef stock, spices, and fresh thyme.

Wash the bell peppers and the chilis, cut them in half, and remove the seeds. Dice the bell peppers and add them to the pot, followed by the halved chilis. Add the chopped tomatoes, tomato paste, and the beans, and let the stew simmer for 30 minutes or longer, until the meat is nice and tender. Add salt and pepper to taste and serve with crème fraîche, lime, red onion, and peanuts on top.

CHICKEN CURRY WITH COCONUT MILK, FRESH CILANTRO & PEANUTS

I love this tasty and beautiful yellow curry dish. I like it when there is a little heat in the curry, but you can decide how spicy you want yours to be by first going easy on the spices and then adding more if needed. To make the soup a creamy consistency, follow the directions below to thicken it.

// INGREDIENTS

4 tablespoons olive oil

1 pound (500 g) chicken breasts, diced

4 scallions

2 yellow onions, chopped

1–3 teaspoons curry powder (or to taste)

2 cups chicken stock

1 teaspoon sugar

1 can unsweetened coconut milk

½ cup heavy cream

3 tablespoons fish sauce (can be omitted)

Salt and pepper

Optional: 3 tablespoons flour and ¼ cup water for thickening the soup

Warm up the olive oil in a pot and add the diced chicken pieces, browning them until they are well done. Alternatively, you can grill the chicken breasts before you cut them into smaller pieces.

Wash the scallions and cut off the stalks. Grill them on a grate until they are charred. Let them cool a little and then slice them.

Let the onion and the curry powder sweat in the pot for a couple of minutes. Add the meat, the scallions, the chicken stock, sugar, and coconut milk, and let the dish cook for 10 minutes. Then add the cream and let simmer for another 15 minutes. Add more curry powder (to taste), fish sauce (optional), and salt and pepper. If you find that the stew is too thin, then add the water and flour mixture to thicken it.

Serve with rice, fresh cilantro, peanuts, and lime.

Tip: Cook the rice at home. When you're ready to serve it, put it in a strainer and pour boiling water over it.

FRIED PLAICE WITH PARSLEY, MELTED BUTTER & SMALL POTATOES

Everyone absolutely loves flat fish made on the campfire. Plaice can be tough to find in the United States, so feel free to substitute sole, halibut, or flounder. Make a fire on the beach on a nice summer's day and try this dish. There is nothing more authentic than cooking fish over an open fire.

// INGREDIENTS

4 cleaned and filleted
    plaice (or sole,
    halibut, or flounder)

Rye flour

Butter

Sunflower oil

Salt and pepper

Small potatoes

Italian flat leaf parsley,
    chopped

Dry the fish with a kitchen towel. Sprinkle both sides of the fish with salt and pepper and turn the fish gently in rye flour. Fry the fish in a skillet on a grate over embers in plenty of sunflower oil and butter, approximately 3 minutes on each side.

Boil the potatoes (this can be done at home) and fry them in butter to give them a crusty surface before serving.

Serve the plaice with the potatoes and sprinkle everything with the chopped parsley.

RUSTIC CAMPFIRE DISH WITH BACON, SOFT ONIONS & PICKLED BEETS

This is a dish that must be part of this book because it epitomizes my love of campfire cooking. The mashed potatoes are rustic and creamy, and with the bacon and soft onions, this simple and delicious dish is a real winner. With the addition of pickled beets, it can't get any better. Yes please!

// INGREDIENTS

2 pounds (1 kg) potatoes

4 tablespoons (50 g) butter

½ cup whole milk

¼ teaspoon nutmeg

Salt and pepper

5 ounces (150 g) bacon, diced

2 yellow onions, sliced

Pickled sliced beets (see recipe on page 177)

Watercress

Chives

Peel the potatoes and cut them into small cubes so that they can be mashed easily with a fork. Boil them in water for 15 to 18 minutes, or until they are soft, and discard the water. Add butter, milk, and nutmeg, and mash the potatoes. Add salt and pepper to taste, and if necessary, add more milk if you like the mash to be a little runnier.

Fry the bacon in the skillet and place it in a bowl when it's cooked through. Then sweat the onion in the bacon fat until it's nicely browned.

Serve this lovely dish with the soft onions, bacon, pickled beets, watercress, and chives.

Tip: Try adding fresh or pickled red onion as a topping.

DESSERTS

FRENCH TOAST WITH BLACKBERRIES & MAPLE SYRUP

This dessert, which can also be served for breakfast, is a hit with all ages. My children are crazy about French toast—or *"Poor Knights,"* as it's called in Danish. If you like to enhance the dish to have as breakfast, you can add crispy bacon on top. This is a great way to get ready for a long walk in the woods, which will help to burn the calories that you enjoyed for breakfast.

// INGREDIENTS

8 slices white bread

3 eggs

2 tablespoons sugar

½ cup milk

A dash of salt

1½ teaspoons ground
   cinnamon

Butter for frying

Toppings

Fresh berries, mint,
   maple syrup, or
   acacia honey

Combine the eggs, sugar, milk, salt, and cinnamon in a bowl and whisk the mixture. Toss the bread in the mixture and fry each slice in butter until it's crispy on both sides.

Serve with fresh berries, mint, and maple syrup, or with acacia honey. Sprinkle with a little extra cinnamon if you like.

WAFFLES WITH BLACKBERRY JAM, FRESH BERRIES & MINT

The smell and taste of waffles made on a campfire are hard to beat, and they are a lot of fun to make. Remember to use plenty of butter to stop the waffles from burning. It can be difficult to avoid, but with more butter in the waffle iron, you're less likely to end up with a burned waffle.

// INGREDIENTS

3½ cups (300 g) flour

3 teaspoons baking powder

Seeds from 1 vanilla pod, or 2 teaspoons vanilla extract

2 tablespoons sugar

2 cups whole milk

½ teaspoon salt

3 eggs

5 tablespoons (75 g) butter, melted

Sunflower oil for greasing the waffle iron

Butter for frying

Toppings

Powdered sugar, fresh raspberries, mint, toasted hazelnuts, and maple syrup

Combine all the ingredients well (except for toppings).

Pour 1 teaspoon sunflower oil evenly into the waffle iron and heat the iron over the fire to help keep the batter from sticking to the iron. Add a little butter to further grease the iron and pour in the waffle batter. Grill the waffles over the embers until they are crispy on both sides. Keep turning the iron and make sure that they don't burn. The waffle iron is heavy and it's therefore a good idea to place it on top of a grate.

Sift powdered sugar over the waffles, then add fresh berries, mint, toasted nuts, and maple syrup.

Tip: Make the waffle batter at home and store it in a bottle.

MARSHMALLOW SANDWICH WITH POMEGRANATE & CARAMEL SAUCE

Who can toast the most marshmallows before dinner? When my boys were little, we often toasted marshmallows, and sometimes even before dinner, which certainly wasn't "proper." But after all, outdoor rules are different from indoor rules. Perhaps you could have a competition for the best or the craziest marshmallow sandwich? A perfect toasted marshmallow has a crispy surface all around and is moist inside. This dish is the "Crème Brûlée" of campfire cooking and needs to be grilled slowly over the embers. You may be tempted to grill the marshmallows directly on the flames but watch out; if you do this, the marshmallows will become crispy. The acidity of the apples and the pomegranates work well to balance the sweetness of the marshmallows.

// INGREDIENTS

1 bag marshmallows

1 apple, sliced

2 tablespoons pomegranate seeds

Salted caramel sauce (see recipe on page 155), or you can use chocolate sauce

1 packet of your favorite cookies

Grill the marshmallows on sticks that have had the bark peeled off. The marshmallows should be grilled slowly over the embers to avoid burning.

Make the marshmallow sandwiches by starting with a slice of apple, then follow with a marshmallow, a cookie, and finish the sandwich with caramel sauce and pomegranate seeds.

Tip: Let the marshmallows cool down just a bit before you eat them. A very hot marshmallow can burn your tongue.

CINNAMON BUNS ON A STICK

The smell of cinnamon and brown sugar on a campfire is fantastic. These cinnamon buns on a stick can be a little tricky to make. The key is not to make them too big, and not to overfill them so that they don't fall off the stick while they are cooking. This will be an exercise in patience for the cook. It's even more important to cook these buns slowly over the embers because otherwise the sugar may burn, and the buns end up with a bitter taste. Make sure that you have enough dough so that you can make an extra bun just in case you have an accident. If you can't find fresh yeast, you can use about 3 teaspoons active dry yeast instead. Just make sure the milk is warm (but not hot) to activate the yeast properly.

// INGREDIENTS

3½ tablespoons (50 g) butter

1¼ cup milk

1 ounce (30 g) fresh yeast
    (or see note above
    about active dry yeast
    substitute)

½ teaspoon salt

2 teaspoons sugar

3 cups + 2 tablespoons
    (500 g) flour

Filling

½ cup (120 g) butter

⅔ cup (120 g) brown sugar

2 teaspoons ground
    cinnamon

Glaze

¾ cups (100 g) powdered
    sugar (approximately)

2–3 teaspoons water

Melt the butter in a skillet and add the milk. Pour the butter and milk mixture into a bowl and stir in the yeast. Add the sugar and flour and mix well. Cover it with a tea towel and leave it to rise for 30 to 60 minutes.

Make the filling by combining the softened butter with the brown sugar and cinnamon.

Make the glaze by placing the powdered sugar in a bowl and then adding 2 teaspoons water. If the glaze is too thick, add a little more water.

Divide the dough into 10 parts and use a rolling pin to make 8 rectangles measuring approximately 3 x 8 inches. Place the filling on top of each rectangle using a knife to spread it out evenly. Make sure that there is a ¼ to ½-inch edge all around the rectangle that is left without filling. Roll the rectangle lengthwise until it resembles a sausage that can be skewered on the stick. Grill the cinnamon buns slowly over the embers until they are crispy and golden. Avoid cooking the buns directly over the fire because it's easy to burn both the bread and the sugar this way.

Add the glaze to the finished buns.

*Pizza on a stick with pepperoni,
mozzarella & red onion, page 80*

GRILLED PINEAPPLE WITH WHIPPED CREAM, SALTED CARAMEL SAUCE & POMEGRANATE

This is my absolute favorite dessert to make over a campfire, and the one that I pick when there are children around, or when I want to create a very special ending to a good meal cooked over the fire. This dish makes everyone leave with a smile on their face. It's always a winner. The combination of the crispy texture and the acidity of the pineapple with the sweetness of the caramel is perfect. But watch out, you can easily become obsessed with the caramel sauce. . . .

// INGREDIENTS

1 pineapple

Toppings
Whipped cream, salted
    caramel sauce, and
    pomegranate seeds
    (can be omitted)

Cut off the top of the pineapple and stand it upright so that you can cut off the sides. Then cut the pineapple into slices measuring just under 1 inch. Grill them until they become slightly charred and crispy.

Top the pineapple slices with whipped cream, salted caramel sauce, and pomegranate seeds.

SALTED CARAMEL SAUCE

7 tablespoons (100 g)
    butter
½ cup (100 g) brown
    sugar
½ teaspoon salt
1½ teaspoons vanilla
    sugar or 1 teaspoon
    vanilla extract
½ cup heavy cream

Melt the butter and the brown sugar in a skillet over medium heat. Add salt and vanilla. When the brown sugar has melted, add the cream.

BAKED APPLES WITH CINNAMON, RAISINS, BROWN SUGAR, NUTS & WHIPPED CREAM

It's always nice to end a campfire meal with a dessert. Filling an apple with cinnamon, raisins, nuts, and whipped cream is delicious. A perfectly made baked apple is soft with a crispy filling. It's a good idea to pre-cook the apples and grill them after the main course.

// INGREDIENTS

4 apples

1 tablespoon chopped hazelnuts or almonds

2 tablespoons oats

4 teaspoons brown sugar

1 teaspoon ground cinnamon

12 raisins

Foil

Topping

Whipped cream

Make a mixture of nuts, oats, brown sugar, cinnamon, and raisins. Divide the mixture between the apples and pack the apples in foil.

Place the apples directly over the embers and bake them for 8 to 12 minutes. Keep turning them so that they get baked evenly.

Serve the baked apples with whipped cream.

BAKED BANANAS WITH CHOCOLATE CRUMBLE, FRESH MINT, WHIPPED CREAM & WHISKEY

Baked bananas made on the campfire is a classic. The warm banana with melted chocolate and a crispy crumble topping is the perfect ending to a campfire meal. Or make it as a stand-alone dessert for good friends.

// INGREDIENTS

4 bananas

2 tablespoons oats

1 tablespoon brown sugar

1 tablespoon chopped
    hazelnuts

3 ounces (80 g) dark
    chocolate, cut into
    smaller pieces

Foil

Toppings

Whipped cream, fresh
    mint, whiskey

Make a cut with a sharp knife lengthwise on the unpeeled bananas so that you can add the crumble easily. Make sure not to cut through the bananas.

Mix oats, brown sugar, and hazelnuts, and place the crumble in the slit in the bananas. Press down the chocolate on top.

Pack the bananas in foil, making sure that they are completely covered. Bake them over the embers for 8 to 12 minutes, turning them so that they bake evenly. The bananas should be moist with a crispy crumble.

Serve the baked bananas with whipped cream, fresh mint, and perhaps a little whiskey.

Tip: It would be a good idea to make an extra banana that can be used as a tester to check for readiness.

BANANA PANCAKES WITH BLUEBERRIES AND MAPLE SYRUP

Pancakes made on the campfire are always a hit. And if you add bananas, blueberries, and maple syrup as toppings, then you'll most likely be voted best parent of the year. Pour the thick batter into the skillet and add the banana slices into the batter.

// INGREDIENTS

2 cups + 2 tablespoons
   milk

4 tablespoons (50 g)
   melted butter

4 eggs

1 teaspoon salt

2 teaspoons baking
   powder

1 teaspoon vanilla sugar
   or ¾ teaspoon vanilla
   extract

1 teaspoon sugar

2 cups flour

Butter for frying

2 bananas cut into slices

Topping

Blueberries and maple
   syrup

Combine the milk, melted butter, eggs, salt, baking powder, vanilla, sugar, and flour, making sure that there are no lumps in the batter. If the batter is too thin, add a little more flour. The batter should be on the thick side.

Warm up a skillet over the embers and fry the pancakes in butter. Pour the bater in the skillet, making 3 to 5 pancakes at a time. Add 4 to 5 banana slices to each cooking pancake. Fry the pancakes for approximately 1 to 3 minutes on each side.

Serve the banana pancakes with blueberries and maple syrup.

CREPES WITH TOASTED HAZELNUTS, WHIPPED CREAM & RASPBERRY JAM

Who can flip a pancake in the air without it ending up in a tree or on the ground?!

// INGREDIENTS

3 eggs

2 teaspoons sugar

1 teaspoon vanilla
  sugar or ¾ teaspoon
  vanilla extract

½ teaspoon ground
  cardamom

A pinch of salt

1¼ cup whole milk

2 tablespoons (30 g)
  butter, melted

1¼ cups (150 g) flour

Butter for frying

Toppings

Whipped cream

Raspberry jam, toasted
  hazelnuts

Combine the eggs with the sugar, vanilla, cardamom, and salt. Add the milk, melted butter, and flour, and mix well until the batter is nice and smooth. Adjust the consistency by adding flour or milk until the batter is perfect; not too runny, but not too thick.

Warm up a skillet over the embers and add a generous pat of butter. When the butter has melted, add approximately ¼ to ½ cup pancake batter to the pan, depending on the size of the pan. Fry the crepes until they are golden on both sides.

Serve the crepes with whipped cream, raspberry jam, and toasted hazelnuts.

DRINKS

HOT BLACK CURRANT DRINK WITH CINNAMON, STAR ANISE, ORANGE & LEMON

This is the world's easiest and most delicious black currant drink. It's a winner with young and old alike on a cold winter's day by the campfire, but it can also be served on a cool summer's day. If you like, you can add a little bit of rum to the drink if there are no children present.

// INGREDIENTS

4⅓ cups (1 L) black
    currant syrup
3 cinnamon sticks
8 star anise pods
1 mild chili
4 slices lemons
3 slices oranges

Combine all the ingredients in a saucepan, place on a grate over the fire, and simmer for half an hour. Ladle out the liquid into mugs to serve.

IRISH COFFEE WITH WHISKEY, BROWN SUGAR & WHIPPED CREAM

Irish coffee is the perfect ending to a campfire meal. Make a pot of coffee ahead at home or make it fresh by the fire. You can make things easy for yourself and use instant coffee and ready-made whipped cream in a can (you are allowed to take shortcuts), but if you have more time, freshly ground good quality coffee and freshly whipped cream will make this drink even more luxurious.

// INGREDIENTS

For 1 serving of Irish coffee:

1 jigger (1½ ounces, or 3 tablespoons) whiskey

2–3 teaspoons brown sugar

1 cup brewed coffee

Whipped cream

Mix whiskey and brown sugar in a cup. Add one cup coffee and stir. Drop a dollop of whipped cream into the drink and a couple of drops of whiskey on top. Enjoy this warm drink by the campfire with smoke in your eyes in good company.

HOT CHOCOLATE WITH WHIPPED CREAM, COGNAC & TOASTED MARSHMALLOWS

You don't always need to come up with an elaborate campfire menu when you're outdoors. You can easily make a small fire and enjoy a hot chocolate that will warm you from the inside out. If children are present, omit the alcohol.

// INGREDIENTS

1 ounce cognac (omit if
    children are present)
¾ cup hot chocolate
Whipped cream
A couple of toasted
    marshmallows
Grated chocolate

Start by pouring the cognac into a cup and top with hot chocolate, whipped cream, marshmallows, and grated chocolate. Cheers!

CONDIMENTS

PICKLED RED ONIONS

I love pickled red onions. You can buy them ready-made if you are short on time, but it's so much more fun to make them yourself. Pickled red onions go really well with food made over a fire, adding both sweetness and acidity to any dish. Use them freely in salads, in burgers, on toast, etc. And while you're at it, you might as well make pickled beets, too (see the recipe on page 177). Normally you cook beets to pickle them whole, but when you slice them thinly there is no reason to cook them—pickle them raw to make them crunchy with a bite. Yes, please!

// INGREDIENTS

2 red onions

1 portion of pickling
    juice (see recipe on
    page 177)

1 glass pickling jar,
    approximately 1¾ cups
    (400 ml)

Cut the onions in half and slice them thinly. Rinse the glass pickling jar with boiling water and add the sliced onions. Pour the pickling juice over the onions to cover them completely. Let the onions soak, preferably for at least one day before you serve them.

PICKLED SLICED BEETS

// INGREDIENTS

2 red beets

1 portion of pickling
    juice

1 glass pickling jar,
    approximately
    1¾ cups (400 ml)

Peel the beets and cut them into thin slices. Rinse the glass pickling jar with boiling water and add the sliced beets. Cover the beets completely with the pickling juice. Let the beets soak in the juice for at least one day before you serve them.

1 PORTION PICKLING JUICE

¾ cup water

¾ cup vinegar

¾ cup sugar

8 black peppercorns

2 bay leaves

Bring water, vinegar, and sugar to boil. Let cool and pour into the glass pickling jar, covering the pickles. Add peppercorns and bay leaves.

Tacos in
the cam

y appeared on the day when we had a photo shoot
s brave enough to jump inside the stones where
spect! It continued to walk around and pick at
ut the day. It was a funny sight. It clearly enjoyed
ofire food. A good sign!

THANK YOU

I would like to thank everyone who has made it possible for this Campfire cookbook to become a reality. I feel a little nostalgic when I think back at all the good memories I've had by the campfire, both as a child and as an adult.

Thank you to Lars from Eventyrsport, for the cooperation, the sparring, and for your belief in this project. Thanks also to your son Simon for all the help he gave by the campfire. I truly respect the input from you both. Thanks to Jesper and the rest of the team at Forlaget Turbine Publishers for the cooperation and the fantastic service given by you all for the Danish edition of this book. Thanks to my good friend Isabel from Outdoor365 for the cooperation and for your help in inspiring people to go out into nature. Thank you Louise and the team from STM Sport for the cooperation. Thanks to Petromax for providing quality gear. It's very important to have the right equipment when you're cooking outdoors. It makes the experience so much more authentic and convenient. Thank you to Lundhags for providing me with excellent and durable outdoor clothing. Thanks to Jesper Rais for great cooperation and fantastic pictures. Thank you to the very able Liselotte for your energy and help by the campfire, as well as for the food styling. Thanks to my two most delightful helpers, Noah and Kristoffer, who helped make this book happen and for all our amazing times by the campfire and in nature. You make me smile, and you inspire me. Thanks to the illustrator, Jimi Holstebro at Hoedt-Holstebro, for the amazing illustrations. Thanks to my parents who came to visit me by the campfire to give me a hand and to taste the food. Thanks to my good friend Kasper R for chopping wood for the fire, and for grilling the pizza bread on a stick. Thanks to Morten from Lergavsgaard for providing the location. Thanks to Jimmy from Griffenfelds for his support and backing. Thanks to Ronster for the help with graphics. Thanks to my good friend Niller for coming up with the title for the book. Thanks to Elena for being a hand model. Thanks to all my friends with whom I've had fantastic times by the campfire, and who have shared many good stories with me while getting smoke in their eyes. Thanks to Jer who stopped by and contributed to the good atmosphere. Thanks to the brave hen for photobombing our pictures. Thanks to all the good people whom I've met by the campfire throughout the years, and who have inspired me in so many ways. When you're sitting around a fire together you feel free to talk about almost anything. Thanks to Hulk from Trygsen Service, the world's best event planner, who has helped me with lots of campfire events and much more. Thanks to all who stopped by to taste the food by my campfire, and also for your feedback.

Last, but not least, *many* thanks to all who bought this book. I hope that you will have some fantastic times by the campfire with this book.

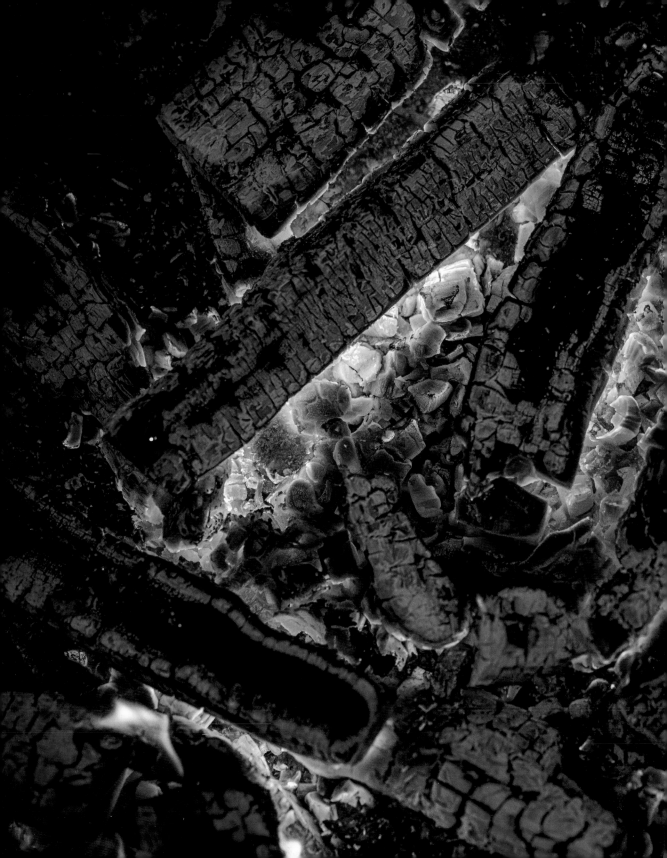

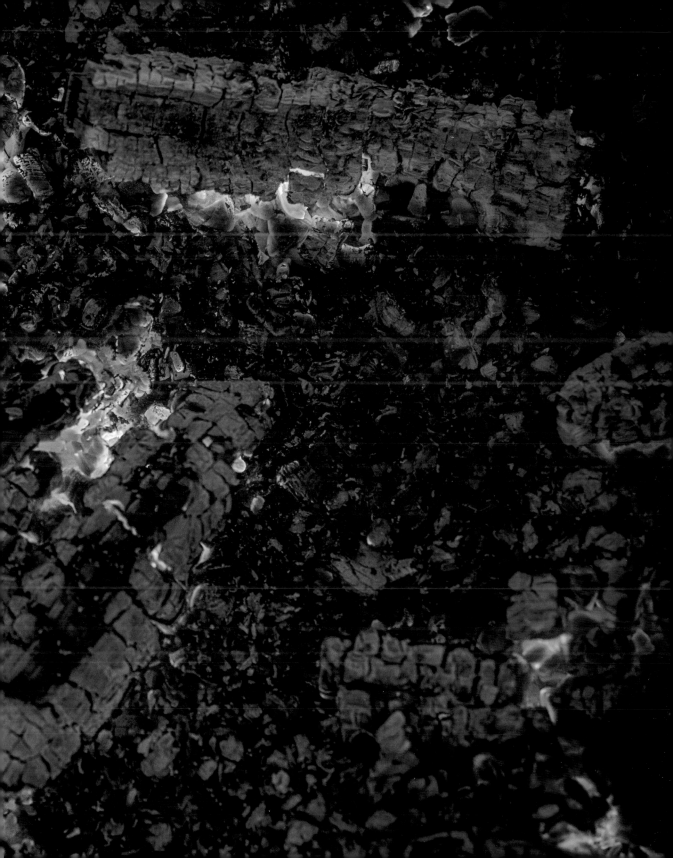